a.k.a. Honey

a.k.a. Honey

◆

An Unauthorized, Early-Years Autobiography

*Florence Mary Marie
Taubman King*

iUniverse, Inc.
New York   Bloomington

a.k.a. Honey
An Unauthorized, Early-Years Autobiography

iUniverse books may be ordered through booksellers or by contacting:

iUniverse
1663 Liberty Drive
Bloomington, IN 47403
www.iuniverse.com
1-800-Authors (1-800-288-4677)

ISBN: 978-0-595-52438-9 (pbk)
ISBN: 978-0-595-62492-8 (ebk)

Printed in the United States of America

iUniverse Rev. 10/29/08

Acknowledgements

Back cover picture of 93-year-old Florence Taubman King appeared December 2004 in the Saint Mary's Annual Church Book.

Contents of this book are taken from a series of letters written by Mrs. King beginning in the year 2000.

Thanks to Will, Kimberlee, Barry, Gail, Bev and Jere, Lorraine, Mary, Carol Lacy, and all for help putting together this book.

1

2001-Merry Christmas

So I've made my ninetieth Thanksgiving. With a little luck and God's will, I'll make my ninetieth Christmas. Isn't that almost unbelievable?

I really don't know why I'm revealing all the sins of my past life. Maybe I should give this to the priest—longest confession in his life, and he's not young.

I will admit to you that I was born March 13, 1911, in a haunted house on Bible Hill in Shell Lake, Wisconsin. I came into the world screaming and continued to do it for three months. I was the fifth birth to Hedwig (Rosenow) Taubman and Frank Taubman. The first child was a son, Lawrence, born March 2, 1900, in Bryant, South Dakota. The second a daughter, Verna Christena, who died at age two years and is buried in the Bryant Cemetery. Jere Probert and I restored the grave markers in 1995 or '96. The third child, a girl, was named Verna Verneta Zepora. She grew up feeling she was the replacement of Verna, but no daughters ever really replaced Verna in our mother's heart. She was the dearest, most beautiful, etc. The fourth child (female) was named Ruth and was a frail member of the clan. She contracted tuberculosis while in high school. It seemed there was almost an epidemic there at that time. Out of five or six in the community who caught it, she was the only one to survive, and lived to seventy-something. Born 1-29-09, I think.

Lawrence, Ruth and Verneta

Tuberculosis was not new to us. My father had a sister who had it, although I never met her or contacted her. Then I came screaming into the world (Ruth and I both born in Shell Lake). Verneta, by then, was about six years old and the story goes that the blue crib built by our father, and which served four children, had to have rockers put under it for me. Verneta lay on the floor under it and rocked with her hands or feet. In one instance she overdid herself and dumped me on the floor. The rockers later were removed and my next memory of it was when I was about twenty and Verneta was coming home with her firstborn and Frank and Hedwig's first grandson. The crib was brought from a large storage room on the second floor of the farmhouse Frank had built for his family. (The lumber came from the 160 acres he had bought between Shell Lake and Sarona on Hwy. B, known as the old narrow gauge, once a railroad for loggers to send cars full of logs to S.L. to the sawmill where Frank T. once worked. It was run by an Indian name Larson.) The crib… oh, yes, the crib… was brought out and thoroughly scrubbed. The ticking was laundered and hung in the sun to dry. Fresh, sun-drenched, dried cornhusks were put in, and, with work-worn fingers and much love and pride, the ticking was sewed shut. It was fluffy and thick and smelled so good. The baby was named Frank after his grandpa. Nothing was too good or too much trouble. But the young Frank (three or six months old?) was not impressed. The dry husks rattled and he was of the generation of store-bought mattresses and he rebelled lustily at the noisy thing.

The Newel house on the road between Shell Lake and Spooner are my first memories of home. I was between two and five years of age. I remember the Harrington School where the big kids went. I remember the geese spreading their wings and stretching their long necks and chasing me, and the turkey gobbler spreading his tail, gobbling and strutting, looking mean as Moses. I learned to run pretty fast. The yard belonged to the feathered creatures. There was meat for feasting and down for feather beds and pillows.

I remember a playhouse in the attic of the small shed where the big kids pushed me up and let me sample Ma's dandelion wine so I wouldn't snitch on them…I still like dandelion wine, but who makes it?

I remember Papa bringing groceries home from town in the egg crate that had twelve dozen eggs in it when he left home. Mr. Taylor, the Indian who operated the store, always put a little bag of candy in with the groceries. I also remember the day he quit doing that. We always assumed Papa bought the candy. Papa's stocks took a mighty plunge that day. But the tragedy that caused my stock to plunge was the day Lawrence had a hunting accident and shot his left foot full of lead. He was fourteen. I was three. He and his buddy got lost. Lawrence climbed a tree to get a better view. His buddy stumbled over a root and the gun fired. This was the first time in my life that I lost everybody's attention.

They wouldn't even take time to tell me what happened or where everyone was going.

What a horror that was for me! I was devastated to the point of dropping my pants, and even then nobody paid attention! Lawrence had to be transported a hundred miles to Eau Claire to a hospital—I suppose by train, how else in 1915? They operated and cut off all the mangled toes, even the big one which the doctor tried to save. Little shots worked out of that foot years later, but I only remember the day it happened and my tragic loss of prestige.

I remember the spring ride in the buggy when we went into Shell Lake, in one side and out the other. It was a long and delightful adventure. We had no house, only the woods and a Shanty hastily built on four stumps so the house builders had shelter for the night. The builders fell behind schedule and the Shanty became home through the winter. I was five, and Ma home-schooled me, since West Sarona Rural School was three miles away. I sat with my feet in the oven a lot that winter. Chilblains were something you lived with.

The Shanty- Lawrence's children, Lorraine and Beverlee c. 1934-1935

2

The Shanty

It was a spring day in 1915. Mamma, Ruth (age six), and I, Florence (age four), were riding west out of Shell Lake. We traveled the lakeshore road that came from the north to the lumber town of Shell Lake. It was exciting. We seldom were taken to town.

Mamma drove down Main Street to the first crossroad and turned left on the narrow gauge road. The road followed the bed of a narrow gauge railroad built by pioneer lumber men who came to make their fortunes logging. The tracks were laid from Shell Lake and went on for five miles out into the virgin forest, always rising gradually, not noticeable to the naked eye. Skilled engineers filled in swamps and cut a roadway through the hills. Freight cars, called flat cars, were pulled into the forest and turned around at the round house and headed back downhill. The lumber men loaded their virgin timber onto each flat car and then nudged the car; it would gently roll to Shell Lake where the logs were dumped into the lake and the flat car shuttled onto a holding track. This went on until all the flat cars were down. Then the process was repeated until the virgin wood was harvested.

As Mamma and Ruth and I drove down the narrow gauge, Queen, our big farm horse, plodded at a steady but slow gait. The morning sun was now quite high and warmed our backs. Tree branches formed a canopy over the road in places. It was like driving through a tunnel. The second growth woodland was green with beautiful ferns and white with wild trillions. The buggy was loaded with boxes of bedding, clothes, kettles…all it could hold.

WE WERE MOVING TO THE SHANTY!

It was a long trip from five miles north to five miles west of the sparkling, clear spring-water lake. We were never far from the water but seldom close enough to see it. Birds sang. Small animals skittered across the road, resenting our intrusion. We met no traffic and passed only two farms with a barn, a house, and a silo.

We rode safely through the big, filled-in swamp, and through the cuts in the hills. Just before reaching our turnoff we passed a piece of open land on which was a windowless two-story house, black with age and weathering, evidence of failure for any number of possible reasons. In the years ahead we would play in it, pick berries from bushes surrounding it, and disturb the snakes and small forest animals that lived around it. A quarter mile from the second inhabited farm was our drive. Mamma carefully held Queen back, since the road was higher than our land due to it being part of the old narrow gauge built for trains. Queen made the turn and the buggy rattled and rolled as she held it back. About a city block away stood THE SHANTY!! "That's it," we girls screamed together, "there's the Shanty!!" Mother sighed deeply, "That's it." She said no more.

The drive was bumpy, rutted dirt and Mamma was busy trying to guide Queen over the ruts without losing any of our wares. The land we were skirting was Tony Frey's property where the railroad had crossed diagonally through his forty acres. His buildings were not visible due to a hill through which the railroad had cut to keep the track at the proper slant. Years later we would climb Tony's hill in the winter time with a sled, or whatever, and slide down the hill toward home, then up the hill and down again. The Frey kids, seeing us, would come and join us. Leona was Ruth's age and Oliver mine.

We could see the foundation of our new home. It was to be finished by fall, and we would be in and settled before snow flew. That was the plan. Beyond the foundation was the Shanty. Papa and his hired help bunked there while they cleared land and hauled the logs to town and brought back lumber to build the farm. Papa worked at the sawmills when he could, but mostly he and his hired help lived in the Shanty, did chores, picked up rock…Lordy, the rocks! In ten years the small fields were rock bound. The barn was east of the house on a hill. It held six milk cows and four horses. The hay was stacked in the barnyard.

Papa bought eighty acres because Uncle Charlie said it was a great opportunity. Uncle Charlie was Papa's brother. He had already bought west of Shell Lake. Papa had lived in Dakota and realized that you had to have big fields to prosper in farming. Land was cheap, so he bought the first eighty acres, forty for each of his two children, Lawrence and Verneta. But Mother Nature controlled life back then and before he could clear land, build a barn, and buy cattle, he had two more daughters to support. So he bought the adjoining eighty acres. None of it was under plow or even cleared of timber. Most of the 160 acres were weed land and pasture. But Papa was confident and Mamma trusted him—he was a college man, a harness shop man with a knee-length college coat made of fur! Papa was used to South Dakota where, with the naked eye one could see for miles, where wheat fields covered acre after acre. He was now a pioneer in this lake, swamp, and lumber country.

Queen stopped behind the house foundation, she was home and ready for her reward. Ruth and I scrambled off the loaded buggy and Queen was watered and turned loose to pasture. We danced and squealed, and acted like two wild geese honking about. We had never seen anything like this!

We raced to the Shanty, our summer home. Ruth was taller and leaner and more agile than I; I still hadn't shed all my baby fat, so I came panting behind. With perfect abandon we explored the area. We could crawl under the Shanty like the dog did, or go up on the flat roof and yoo-hoo to see if we could get an echo. Papa's echo quickly reached us and we hurried down. When Papa was around, we knew better than to play deaf. He never spanked but instinct told us it was wiser to shape up than to find out if he ever would.

The flat-roofed one-room Shanty stood a foot or two off the ground, its corners anchored to four tree stumps. Papa, with his level, had seen to it that each was the right height so the wide board floor was level. It had kitchen-sized windows to the north and south. On the east end a lean-to had been built with wide planks of green lumber. During the summer the planks dried apart, leaving cracks big enough to stick our fingers through. Snow often covered the beds. Sometimes when there were too many for the beds I got to sleep in the Shanty part—where the stove was—on an old, wide, homemade ironing board. Each end rested on a chair and a straight-backed chair along the edge kept me on it. (I was five, I suppose. It must have been 1916.) I had no problems. I had the best there was.

The Shanty – Ruth and Florence (or possibly Verneta) February 1922

Papa and his help began unloading the buggy. Mamma was inside trying to make a home out of the Shanty. There was a cook stove and a heater, planks on sawhorses for a table. A door led into the sleeping room—no floor there, other than Mother Nature's. Papa had the cabin pretty well stocked with basic food. He cooked for the boys who helped him; young growing boys would work for a good meal or two, and they had hearty appetites. Now we were all hungry and Mamma took over. Ruth and I set the table. We spoke very little and were ready for bed as soon as the dishes were done, and were asleep by the time Mamma got us tucked in.

We were spending our first night in our summer home—
THE SHANTY.

3

Verneta, by then, was in sixth grade and was "boarded out" among friends to finish the year in Harrington Rural School between S.L. and Spooner. She remained there through seventh grade. I really never remembered her as my sister until she got married and came home with her family.

The next fall I started school at the West Sarona Rural, a one-room school with eight grades and one teacher. Having been taught at home I was too smart for first grade and caused a problem for the teacher, so I was put in second grade. All my school years I felt I missed something vital by that act. (In my thirty-some years of teaching first graders I don't think I ever let one skip a year or half a year.) Memory work, study habits, or something, never developed properly. School did not come easy for me and grades were nothing to brag about.

Pa managed, in three years, to create a new school district and have a rural school built on an acre of land in the woods across the road from our farm. WWI was in full bloom then. I cut flannel pen wipers to help the soldiers while in the second grade. Everyone contributed. In third grade in our new Oak Grove school we were chanting:

Old Kaiser Bill went up the hill

To take a look at France.

Old Kaiser Bill came down the hill

With a bullet in his pants.

By then I was aware of my German heritage. I grew up thinking my name was "Honey" since "Florence" was too much like "Lawrence." I was in high school before I ever answered to Florence and I felt like a foreigner. But in the days of Kaiser Bill other slogans were created, like: "Hon, Hon, you son of a gun" ("Hun, Hun…"). As a result Ruth and I took on a couple of neighbor kids who were smaller than me and also of German descent, but the Huns were the ones we were fighting. Ruth and I lost the battle and got rolled off the road down a stone pile with a few bruises and a horribly deflated ego. By the next day we were good friends again. I had a mud fight with the male character of that pair once. We were in the same grade. I don't recall what that was about but it happened while playing baseball. I went home for dinner and refused to change clothes 'cause I was going to finish that fight. As I crossed into the schoolyard my enemy greeted me with a wide smile and said, "Come on, Honey. You're on my team," and there ended my revenge.

Lawrence, being eleven years older than me, was chomping at the bit to "go fight the Huns." But at fourteen he had a hunting accident and lost all toes off one foot. It was a horrible burden to bear. All his Taubman male cousins were overseas and he never got to go.

I remember the Ransoms, lifelong friends of Papa and Mamma. They lived next door to us in the Newel house. It seemed I spent quite a lot of my preschool days at this house. There was a banister, slick and smooth, coming from upstairs. I loved to keep it shiny by sliding down it, much to Julia's distress. Julia and Ed had raised two daughters. Ruth and I inherited their lovely dolls and doll clothes and a doll trunk to keep them in. Verneta somehow rescued the unique trunk, which eventually was demoted to her garage attic where it deteriorated and gathered dust until she died in 1995. It had to be close to a hundred years old by then. Its interior was most amazing with a lovely lady's face in the cover. It was rescued once again from the trash pile and stands open on my nephew's living room table with antique family pictures and lace doilies, etc., draped on it. Julia, who was quite the lady, would be delighted and Ed Ransom, who was a portly, jolly character, would have a chuckle.

Julia and Ed and Papa and Mamma all spent their last years back in Shell Lake and played cards together, sharing a lifetime of memories. Of course, Julia and Ed were older and socially quite a few notches above the Taubmans. After all, they were firmly established and Mamma and Papa were pioneers to the northern Wisconsin woodland. The Ransoms were farmers well established. Mamma and Papa had to cut trees, pull stumps, and clear their land.

Shell Lake retirement home – Florence, Hedwig, Frank and Ruth

Our Shanty in the forest was ten miles from our old community. To continue our social life meant an all-day trip by horse and buggy, so we seldom communicated with old neighbors. Uncle Charlie had already moved back to Minnesota and we were alone in the woods. There was no sound but the whinny of horses, mooing of cows, or clucking of chickens and the rooster crowing. And there was always work. The new house was never like the Dakota house, but such an improvement over the Shanty.

I remember the sleeping porch upstairs on the east end of the house, and the tall white pine that stood nearby. The wind sang through the branches, which were at our level on the second floor. There was no ceiling, just the unfinished roof. When it rained it was wonderful! Rain on the roof! The wind and the rain and the morning sun. It was a luxurious way to camp out. Cornhusk mattresses beneath and featherbeds above! Could heaven improve on this?

The new farm house – the Taubman family

4

Oak Grove Rural School was built near our farm just off the narrow gauge dirt road. My father, Frank Taubman, was instrumental in having it built. He was clerk of the district and hired and fired teachers. Mom boarded the teachers. Having a live-in teacher had its advantages and disadvantages. I once thought it a joke to terrorize the teacher by returning after dismissal to pick up forgotten homework. I entered through a basement window that was located by the stairs so I had no problem entering. I proceeded to lumber up the stairs making gruesome noises. When I opened the door and, rollicking with mirth, made my clever entrance, I found a teacher practically petrified, and I learned that fear was not funny. Mother made clear to me the possible outcomes of such humor right down to "dropping dead."

Apologizing was not a popular thing back in those days. I don't recall ever hearing anyone say, "I'm sorry." We were sorry and ashamed and acted sorrowful, but I had to wait eighty years before the words became popular. Then our President was sorry we killed the Germans, and the Pope was sorry we didn't defend the Jews, the Wild Life group apologized to the animals we skinned to make fur coats, the rich apologized to the poor as they sought new sophisticated ways to make millions, and how we apologized to the Blacks for causing them to have such a lousy life! And, through all our love-love, love-hate, went on a wild rampage. Everybody feared everybody, trusted no one, carried loaded guns and shot on sight, even six-year-old children.

But in my youth I went to a rural school (best system America ever had), milked cows, picked strawberries, and loved my big brother. Father was stern and worked hard clearing land, planting and harvesting, and building buildings. Everyone was expected to contribute according to their age and ability. I was never physically punished and only threatened once when I knew I had it coming. I was putting on an act because I didn't get my way. Ma and Verneta took the horse and buggy and went somewhere, leaving Ruth and me at home. I was too big to cry, but that didn't stop me. Pa pulled his belt and my tears dried up. Close! Very close! My respect for Pa lasted 'till he closed his eyes in death and he died instantly while working—fixing a screen door. He was a faithful father to the end, and I knew it even though we never said, "I'm sorry," or, "I love you."

Life was good. We were progressive farmers. We had the first tractor, the first car (Model T), the first dairy barn to have water piped in for the cows. Eventually we even had a tank in the washroom, which we pumped full when the engine was running. This was for washing up—dishes, cleaning, etc. Fresh water to drink was in a bucket with a dipper. That wasn't always so fresh either. We didn't know what ice water was.

Ma suffered the pangs of poverty because her life in Bryant, South Dakota, was a fancier and more leisurely life. I was a married woman before I got to Bryant and saw the houses Dad and Uncle Bill Boettcher had built for their brides. Side by side stood two beautiful two-storey, square, white houses. Ma's was vacant and the door stood open. There was a huge gracious front entry with a lovely staircase leading upstairs. The hardwood floors still glistened. Eaves caught the water and carried it to the cistern. There was a bathroom! (I didn't know about bathrooms 'till I went to high school, and I didn't have the use of one until I went to college, September 1928.) How did Ma ever survive a winter in the Shanty?

Ma never complained and was always cheerful—basically. Once or twice I recall finding her sitting doing handwork and tears were in her eyes, which she quickly dried. In our attic adventures in the new house, Ruth and I discovered a lock of fine light hair, carefully tied together. For mature women it was known as a "switch" and was used to style coiffures of grandeur. But this was definitely infant hair, shiny and like silk. It was about ten inches long—obviously grown from birth 'till death. Then there were little red-laced shoes and matching stockings. They were never brought out or talked about to anyone that I was aware of. I, in my youth, talked her into having the shoes bronzed—in those days it was something new going on, and I've forgotten details—but a small picture of the original photograph was held by the bronzed shoes. Lorraine Roush may have it. I was never a "keeper."

There was also a large oval-shaped picture that bulged out—fine photography of an infant girl. This was our sister whom only Lawrence had ever seen, and in the big heavy albums were pictures of him and Verna Christena. Verna Verneta Zepora was the second daughter, and all her life (dying at age ninety) felt she was not an entity unto herself but a replacement of Verna. I think it influenced and shaped her whole life. Ruth and I eventually followed but, of course, had there been ten daughters none would have filled the void caused by the death of Verna Christena. She was buried in the cemetery at Bryant, South Dakota. A metal plate covered her tiny grave. A hole about the size of a dinner plate was at one end of the plate and a spirea shrub was planted there; on the rest of the plate was written:

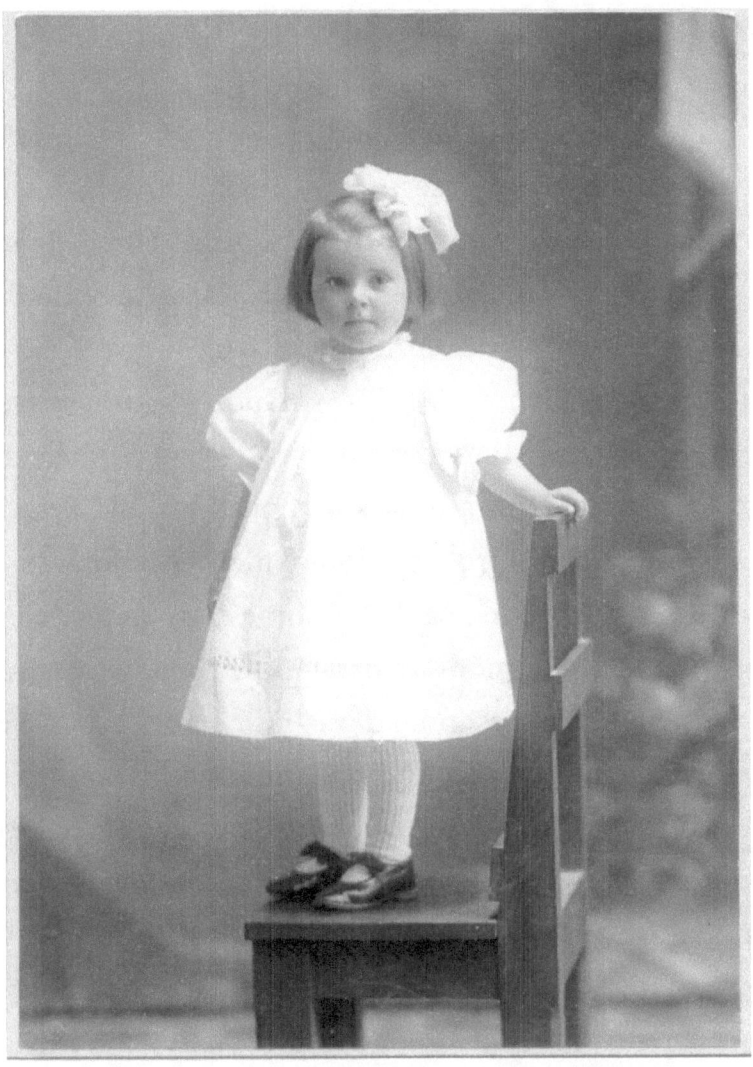

Verneta at about twenty-seven months, the same as Verna when she died; taken because they had no equivalent photo of Verna, according to the notation

Verna Christena Taubman
Born May 9, 1901   Died Aug. 15, 1903
Our Darling

This, and a very tender part of her heart, Mother left in Dakota when they moved to Wisconsin. Each Memorial Day she sent a few dollars to her sister Marie Boettcher or to the Guses to use for upkeep.

In June 1994, when I was 83, I had my first opportunity to visit Bryant and find the tiny grave. Jere Probert and I made a special trip from Madison, South Dakota, where we were visiting Denise Probert Bloom and her family. It stood alone, broken and lonely looking. Some distance away, but in the same area, stood monuments to other family members— grandparents and aunts and uncles, but no one close to Verna. I wondered if Ma and Pa had bought a family plot and still possessed it. I contacted the cemetery and they agreed to put a concrete slab on the grave and anchor the metal cover to it for a very nominal price, which I asked them to do. I also advised them to sell the surrounding plots if they were held by our parents, using the money for cemetery maintenance. We checked the work on a later trip. It was satisfactory, but I never did find out if there were Taubman lots near her grave to be sold.

5

Rural Life in Northern Wisconsin

Papa left Dakota because of poor health. He blamed the water. Cars had put an end to his harness shop. His favorite story of the Dakotas was of a cyclone that passed through and uprooted a huge tree in front of his shop. (He had a picture of himself holding the head of a team of horses in front of his shop.) We had a two-foot section of the tree varnished with casters under it and used it for a footstool; a reminder of bygone days.

The Frank Taubman Harness Shop, Bryant, South Dakota

Papa, for all his poor health, was a worker. He never had time to sit down except to eat. He never walked, he ran—down the hill to the barn and up the hill to the house. He liked time-saving machinery. He had an engine to pump water while the neighbors pumped by hand. He had water in the barn and later in the house. Not running water, just a tank near the ceiling in the washroom with a pipe running from the pump house to the tank. The washroom had a sink with a bucket below. Papa had foresight enough to put a concrete floor in the little four-by-six room. The bucket under the sink was big, and when it was full or running over it was surprising how long one basin of water could last! It had to be carried through the kitchen to the outside door and across the porch and out. Drinking water still had to be hand pumped, carried in and set on a shelf made for it. M-m-m, was that good! Fresh from the well and cold. (Papa's water in Bryant could never have tasted like this.) So they had running water, caught from the roof and heated, and piped through the house. We had a reservoir on the end of the wood-burning kitchen stove, and teakettles and boilers to heat more when needed. On Saturday night Mamma put the round wooden tub at the end of the stove, put in warm water, and Ruth and I got our hair washed and bodies bathed. I don't know if any of the rest of the family used the same water or not, but water was not an item to waste in those days on the farm. How Ma emptied the tub I have no idea. Perhaps it was saved for scrubbing floors.

The Shanty, the new house and the overhead water system

Wisconsin water must have cured Papa's health problems. He rose early, worked long days, never rested, had no time for frivolities, yet I never knew him to be sick-a-bed a day in my life, or go to a doctor, or be in a hospital, or take a pill. He dropped dead at 70-something while working on the screen door in their Shell Lake home.

Since Papa was a two-year college man, and Mamma didn't finish her fourth grade reader, it was Papa's job to help with homework. At night, by the light of the kerosene (Aladdin) lamp, he helped me with my math. While I struggled to follow the directions in the book he worked them in his head, carpenter style. I guess I caught the idea, since math was my favorite subject. English grammar was my downfall. I flunked it in eighth grade county exams and was flunking it in college when, to my relief, my very strict grammar teacher broke her leg and my literature teacher finished the year for her. (One man's loss is another man's gain!) After Mamma died I found her fourth grade reader. I was a teacher then and I'd challenge any high school student to read it. It was not a fourth grade reader of fairy tales, believe me. I wish I knew where it is now—but then I'm not a "keeper."

By 1928 Ruth and I were graduates from Shell Lake High School. Ruth lost time due to poor health, so we graduated together. She missed part of that school year and we took her out of bed for graduation night. Papa and Mamma dropped us off at school and they went to the doctor's office to confer with old Doc Herring (who had brought both Ruth and me into the world) on the subject of Ruth's health problem. Sputum samples had been mailed to University State Hospital in Madison, WI. The results were now available. Papa and Mamma got back in time for our graduation exercises. Mamma had made each of us our lovely voile dresses, but even the lovely dress did little for Ruth. She was sick. The verdict was TB positive. It was not a graduation to be celebrated. Papa went home and started screening in half of the downstairs porch (under the upstairs one) for an outdoor bedroom for

Ruth. Later he built a porch across the front of the house. She slept out there.

Life for the whole family was TB-centered. Mamma and Papa were devastated. I was sworn to see to her care should they not survive to care for her. It was obvious that I must get further educated to be prepared to take over my obligations. This was not a two-week disease. It would be years, actually a lifetime. Papa knew this, for his sister was a tubercular.

Teaching or nursing were about the only opportunities for women. Nursing was not my line and, of course, I had taken business in high school rather than grammar or Latin, which Verneta had so highly recommended me to take—I should have listened since I had to take grammar in college. I borrowed $100, which was to take me through one year of college. (Gladys Lumberg had done it, so could I!)

Verneta was the only one with a cash income. She had gone to Iowa after her graduation where she lived with the John Duff family on a farm. They were relatives. Zepora (John's wife) was Mamma's sister. All our relatives were rich compared to us.

The John Duff family at the Taubman farm; Zepora in the dark dress,
John on the right

Uncle John said she (Verneta) could go to school in Fayette that summer and he, being on the school board, would give her the teaching job. TB was a family project and Verneta did her part by postponing her wedding 'till December so she could loan me $100 for college.

Peterman School, where Verneta taught

I went to Iowa during the Christmas holiday to witness her marriage. I traveled by train, I suppose, and she must have paid my expenses. There were only two witnesses to the marriage, myself and Bill's friend, Milo. Bill was sick and hardly able to attend his wedding. We all wore street clothes and I can scarcely remember the ceremony. It was short and sweet, but the marriage lasted a lifetime. So it isn't the guest list or the banquet or even the sermon that makes a lasting marriage.

Remember the Great Depression? It was on. Jobs were scarce, wages were low and getting lower. I worked for my board and room, the first year for two old maiden ladies, sisters, who lived together in a big house in Eau Claire and took in renters as well as sewing. I was assigned to keep the coal furnace fed and help with the housework. I learned to eat Cream of Wheat with butter instead of cream. It's good. Try it. They were gentle ladies and one walked with a cane. They sewed for some of the college faculty women. I walked a mile to the college, which was across the Chippewa River— the bridge was the longest, coldest bridge on earth, anyway to my knowledge at that time.

Late in the fall, near Thanksgiving, a Shell Lake man who also attended Eau Claire College, told me he was driving home for the weekend and would I like to go along. I was living in a foreign world—did I want to go home? My gracious employers let me go. So what if it is cold and the car had no side curtains? So what if the radiator leaked and we broke the ice on roadside puddles for refills? So what if I was penniless? I had a ride home for an overnighter with a man from a fine neighbor family, dependable and harmless. I can't remember who else went but I had the back seat and blankets and it was cold, cold, cold. It was only a hundred miles. I suppose it took six hours. My parents were aghast. I doubt that they were lonesome for me. Dad (now that I'm a college woman, Papa is for kids) took me aside and said quietly, "Here is a dollar. You should never travel without money." It was my only trip.

Mamma (Mom, now) made me a peach colored linen dress, tailored. It was lovely and my best dress. All else was leftover high school clothes, mostly made-over hand-me-downs. Mom and Dad also bought me an all wool plaid Chippewa jacket, made in Chippewa Falls just down the river. The best! It was my one and only winter coat. My shoes gave out before the second year was over and I had to spend five dollars for a pair of Red Cross shoes, which didn't fit but I had to wear them. I guess they were a little short, and I have bunions today to show for it.

I learned to drink tea by being curious as to what went on at a YWCA tea party for students and faculty. Once inside I discovered there was nothing to do but stay in line (the room was small) and get your tea and wafers and stand around and talk. I had nothing to contribute since city people (which most were) were not really interested in milk and egg production, only in what type of tableware to use for appearances when serving. My tongue stuck to the roof of my mouth. So I said to myself, "Sip tea and try to look at ease and intelligent." To my surprise the tea didn't actually taste bad, it was the smell I didn't like. Mom often drank tea and I had that disagreeable smell in the back of my throat.

6

So much for '28 and '29. I got my $100. Verneta got her husband. And Ruth began her fight against TB at home. Lawrence and his young wife Mildred and their two small daughters moved into the upstairs. Dad and Lawrence pulled the stairway out and reversed it. Now instead of going up from the dining room it went up from outside. The big bedroom that Ruth and I shared while growing up, and the big porch, became their living quarters. There were two small bedrooms left. The house had no bathroom anywhere and wood and water had to be carried upstairs. Lawrence had a small herd of milk cows to add to Dad's. Their last three children were born in that house. Arrangements changed over the years. Ruth went into state supported sanitariums. We were all tested regularly for TB, even the Iowa branch of the family. Mom and Dad rented, or lived rent-free sometimes, in area houses that were vacant for one reason or another. The population was shifting since the north woods were all cut over. Lumbering was no more. Farmers lost their farms and fortunes. The rich, in desperation, jumped off of the highest places they could climb to—like the top lookout on the Madison Capitol. It was eventually closed off to save lives. The poor just went on being poor; whether there is prosperity or good times, being poor doesn't really change.

How I traveled to and from Eau Claire is only one of the many things I seem to dis-remember. No doubt Papa and Mamma took me in the Model T, or did I go by train? Mamma came to visit me for some parent-student occasion. She came by train. My student "big sister" kept her in her home. I was hoping Mamma wouldn't be wearing her long underwear yet. I think it was the YW girls who assigned a "big sister" to every freshman. I was becoming more appearance conscious, particularly about hair styles. I never had long hair and what I had was definitely the end of the line, like me. I was getting used to running water, but still didn't overuse it. I tried to put a few curves in the ends (of my hair). Feeding the coal furnace was no help and I never washed my head more than once every two weeks. It was considered unhealthy to do so, and bad for the hair.

Verneta had fought all the parental fights, and there were tears and battles royal. She was happy to be out of high school before Ruth and I got in. Somehow her life as a child was not as sheltered as Ruth's and mine. She never lived in the

Shanty. She was left with the Ransoms and the Rybergs back in civilization on the "other" side of Shell Lake to finish the school year. By the time they (Ma and Pa) took her back we had a new house and she had her own bedroom. She lived with us, and we three girls went to the West Sarona school three miles away. She graduated from eighth grade that year. Emma Toraungue, our neighbor's daughter whose family moved from Minneapolis to also experience quiet country living, was in the eighth grade. Spring and fall the four of us went by horse and buggy to West Sarona. We left the horse in a nearby farmer's barnyard while we went to school. It was a one-room building with a heater in back, surrounded by a jacket of metal so we couldn't get burned when we tried to warm up. It was a good place to dry mittens. We carried our lunches in a lard bucket, or whatever Mamma had available with a cover. I was the smart little kid since Mamma taught me much while we stoked the stoves and kept our feet off the floor and nursed our chilblains.

I loved my teacher and, since I was ahead of the other first graders, I suppose I was a real pain to her. The rest of my school years I spent at the foot of the class. School was always hard for me. I think Emma, from the big city, sort of citified Verneta. That was the only year she really lived with us. Emma was a lively one. Klubunders had a "rutabeggy" field which we passed driving home, and Emma sent Ruth and me under the fence to steal some to eat on our ride home. Verneta was style conscious. Long hair was going out, haircuts were coming in. Verneta had beautiful hair that was brushed and coiffed. (I never figured out how she did the puffs over the ears). I remember the battles and tears (from Mamma) when she parted with the long hair. For all that it wasn't too many years later when Mamma cut hers. Long underwear, lipstick, and rouge, all were Verneta's battles. By the time Ruth and I "grew up," all was accepted.

High school was a must for us girls. Lawrence had talked his way out of education after two years of high school. Papa was vulnerable since he needed him on the farm. Now Papa and Lawrence together decided that we girls should have high schooling. Papa found a family of six boys and one girl who would keep Verneta for her help. She seldom came home since she was most useful on weekends. In summers she came home and brought the little girl with her. Shirley was cute but a very ornery little girl since her six brothers teased her so much. By the time we sent her home she was quite a nice child, but next time she came we were back to base one.

By Verneta's junior year she was rebelling against education. Eight years of schooling was considered enough by most area farm families. Some of the "upper crust" sent their eighth graders back to repeat grade eight. I wonder now how the teachers handled that. But the repeat students probably got many privileges, like carrying the water, banking the fire, dusting erasers outdoors, shoveling snow, etc. They could be a big help setting up the stage for Christmas programs, rearranging the rows of desks, which were screwed onto two boards and movable by the row. Anyway, Verneta's rebellion met heavy opposition from father and brother. She was finally deported to Cashton, WI, where Grandpa and Grandma Rosenow—Mamma's parents—lived. They were complete strangers to us and they spoke German. They understood very little English.

I had no special attachment to Verneta, she was a family member, but not a family member. She feared the cows and hated the barn. I'd rather milk cows than wash dishes. We had the same parents but we lived different lives. She went to Cashton.

Ruth entered high school, I the eighth grade in the Oak Grove Rural School. Papa had instigated this progress in education. He had a modern one-room school, with a basement and furnace, and all windows on the north. Big windows. This was the latest development. Papa was up to date. They cleared an acre out of the woods just across the road from our farm. I started third grade there and went through eighth. We could walk home for dinner but usually carried a syrup pail or lard bucket for a lunch pail. We carried water for the school bubbler, no more dippers. Sanitation arrived. We boarded the teacher at our home Monday through Friday. She was usually young and peppy, and Lawrence and Verneta were maturing. The house was abuzz. Ruth and I, still in our long white underwear and long black stockings and hair ribbons, watched and learned. Saturday nights it was nothing for all the neighborhood young folks to walk to someone's home, move the furniture, roll up the rug—if there was one, scatter shaved wax on the floor, dance all night, and walk home in daylight, milk the cows, and go to bed. Sunday, the day of rest! Assuming, of course, that there was no hay to get in before rain.

We had a hardwood living room floor, and sometimes the neighbors partied at our house. Old man Siger fiddled on his violin and Wagoner brought his accordion. Papa called the square dances and round dances, and he taught Ruth and me to square dance. I don't remember Mamma dancing, but surely she did. Sometimes Mamma and Papa took us to the Modern Woodmen Hall in Shell Lake and Papa would dance with me. I was probably ten or eleven. Lawrence liked to go to dance halls and dance with all the pretty girls. His one-half empty shoe turned up at the end of his stub foot, but it didn't slow him down, and the girls didn't seem to mind.

Family friend, Frank, Lawrence, Ruth, Hedwig, Verneta, and Florence

7

Papa was always first in the neighborhood to modernize things. He soon gave up the pump handle for a gas engine and pump jack. Then he put drinking cups in the barn, one between every two cows. No more driving the cattle from the barn, through snowdrifts, rain, mud, hail, etc., to the big water tank that had to have a thawing device if the ice was thick. There was no electricity, so how it was done I can't say. It was never my job. Keeping chicken water liquid, that was for me to figure out. By fifteen or so I could crank the engine, holding one hand over the exhaust so it would suck in gas, spin it till it took off full speed, and get the crank off the shaft so it wouldn't spin too and eventually fly off in unpredictable directions. There was a window in line with the shaft and I had visions of someday seeing the crank go out that way. If any person or animal would be in line, they'd never know what hit them. It never happened. Now, if someone hand-pumped a bucketful for a fresh drink in the house, it was necessary to get the belt back on the shaft of the running engine motor, give it a half twist like a figure eight, then deftly run it onto the wheel of the pump jack—first, of course, putting the pump jack in position on the pump rod and securing it with a bolt through the holes provided, if you could get them to line up right. Of course, you've taken the pump handle off the pump rod…right? That's right, if you expect the pump rod to go up and down and send water into the pail, hopefully hanging solidly on the spout where the water comes out. It was a clever idea to have that done before you put your figure eight belt on the pump jack wheel.

In winter there was usually quite a bit of ice underfoot. After all, nothing is perfect. So now it's time to run the belt onto the pump jack wheel in a figure eight. The engine is running smoothly, the belt is on it, the figure eight is made, and now comes the tricky part. You have to run the belt onto the pump jack wheel, and the wheel begins to turn. This wheel is much bigger than the one on the engine that is the source of power. Now if the crank is off and lying at your feet, and you still have five fingers on both hands, you can still get into the action by slipping on the ice and falling into the engine, or the belt, or the pump jack. It's better to play it safe and not dance a victory dance. Enjoy the sound of sweet, cold well water hitting the bottom of the bucket. When it is full, carefully turn off the engine and quickly run the belt off the engine shaft while it slows down. Once it stops completely with the belt still on both wheels you will have to turn the wheel by hand and run the belt off. Carry the bucket into the kitchen, grab the dipper, if someone else isn't already standing there, dipper in hand, waiting for the first dip; in which case you may have to line up and wait your turn. All those people who weren't thirsty when Mamma suggested a fresh pail had dried out in a hurry. For one bucketful one usually pumped by hand. There was always a choice. The well was drilled in front of the Shanty, and eventually a shed extended from the Shanty over the well. The lean-to sleeping porch was eventually improved and was used to shelter our new Model T Ford.

Papa liked to be modern, and his pride of owning a fine looking horse and carriage switched swiftly as he read in his daily paper about Ford's cars. Now, Papa knew the Wright brothers personally by name. Progress was in his blood, though he didn't believe the Wright brothers would ever truly fly. But a car was a great improvement over a horse. He'd save a lot of time going to town once a week, or more often if the mower or plow broke down in the field.

Papa was definitely for saving time and accomplishing more. He'd hardly warm the chair at the dining table unless the horses needed a rest. You had to cool the team and not give them too much water right away, and let them eat their oats and munch a little grass. Papa was not for sitting around and talking. If the horses had to have a noon hour, Papa could pile wood or fix harness. Since he'd once had a harness shop in Bryant, South Dakota, it was nothing new to him. So, when Lawrence drove in with a new Model T Ford, it came as a big surprise.

8

Papa was the first in the neighborhood to have a car! He was hotly reprimanded by our neighbor whose fence divided our land from his. Any man who would let his young son learn to drive the car first was a G.D. idiot. So Lawrence taught Papa to drive! The Ford went thirty-five miles an hour! Such speed! It was black and the top folded down. If it rained we put the top up and buttoned on the side curtain. It had a windshield wiper you could operate by hand from inside. The tires had inner tubes filled with air. If you got a flat tire, and it was just a small nail leak, you might have to just fill the inner tube with air. There was a valve on the inner tube and a burr on the end of the tire pump hose that fit the valve perfectly. A bigger leak took more work.

Under the back seat were tools. You took out the jack and put it under the axle and jacked the car up 'till it was free of the ground. Other tools called "tire irons" were under the seat. With their aid you pulled the tire off, took the tube out and found the leak. If you were close to a cow tank, that was a good place to submerge the tube, section by section, until air bubbles appeared, signifying a leak. Under the back seat with the tools was a little can with patches. The lid of the can was like Mamma's little grater. You used the grater part of the lid to clean and roughen the rubber. Inside the can were sheets of patching and a tube of glue or cement. With scissors you cut off a piece of patching the size you needed, spread a light layer of glue on the tube, let it set up for a bit, then pull the white layer off the piece of patch. Underneath the layer the black rubber was sticky. You pressed the patch over the leak. It adhered instantly. You put the tube back in the tire, and hung the tire over the wheel, lining up the valve with the hole in the rim. You might have to press the stem in the middle of the valve to release some of the air to get the tube in the tire. Using the tire irons you worked and sweat 'till you got the tire back on the wheel. Once the tire was on, you attached the tire pump to the valve and filled the inner tube. You took the jack off by reversing the jacking, or if it was easier, you pushed the car off the jack. You carefully picked up all the tools and the jack, put them under the seat, replaced the seat, and away you went.

Flats happened quite often. Roads were built for horses and buggies. They were rough and rutted in places. Shell Lake had a sandy shore line. One time I turned the wheel on a curve and rolled the tire off. The tire kept right on going down the road ahead of the car. I had to get out and chase it and roll it back. And there on the hot sand in the hot sun with a sandy base for the jack I had to put it back on.

The radiator had to be filled often. The engine started when you stood in front and cranked it with the crank beneath the radiator. On the column that held the steering wheel were two levers sticking out just far enough to move up and down with your fingertips when your hands were on the wheel. The left one was for the spark, the right one fed the gas. You'd better know how to adjust them before you cranked. If you didn't, the crank could kick and break your arm or bang your face into the radiator cap, depending upon how tall you were or how you stood. If it reacted properly the motor would start with a roar and you would race to the side of the car and adjust the two levers and then get in and drive. There were three pedals on the floor which, when properly used, put the car in motion forward, backward, or stopped all action. The brake wasn't too dependable and the first time I, untaught, took the car and ran to town for a loaf of bread (no one was home to tell me not to), the brakes didn't function at all. As I headed toward the intersection (Main Street) a truck beat me to it. I hit the brakes, which gave no response, and coasted on into the last foot of the truck bed. It was scary for me but no one else paid any attention. I drove home carefully.

One of the nicest things about a Model T was that anyone who understood the use of a screwdriver and a wrench could take it apart and put it together again. This was Lawrence's favorite toy, and I was allowed to hold the nuts and bolts in a pan. Of course, Lawrence liked to show off and take the girls for rides. Once he wrecked it and that was another emotional family episode. Somehow he and Mabel got to our house. No one was seriously hurt, but all very emotionally disturbed. Just before his wedding day (he was marrying Mildred) he had an appendectomy and almost died. He was a great guy and helped to raise us girls, but he had his days of glory, if you could call it that, when all the family gave him one-hundred percent of their attention.

Papa drove the Model T down the narrow gauge road, which in lumbering days was a railroad. Rail cars were pulled uphill into the forest. Logs were loaded and as a car was filled it was cut loose and would roll down the sloped tracks five miles to Shell Lake where it ended at the saw mill on the lake shore. Here the logs were dumped into the lake. If this was a fairytale I was gullible enough to always believe it.

Our farm was all second growth timber. The road had a corduroy base. It was cut through the hills and built up in low areas. Anyway, Papa would carefully pull over his fine Model T as far as he dared and turn off the motor if an oncoming team of horses showed any signs of nervousness. In the city, like Chippewa Falls, if he passed a buggy he would nod and tip his hat. What a glorious era it was, the change from horse power to cars! Papa's harness shop in Bryant was soon forgotten, or at least put to rest for life, but the footstool tree trunk remained as evidence of Dakota days.

9

Next Papa had to have a tractor. More land could be put under the plow, a bigger barn could be built, more cows could be milked. Actually, the cows in the new barn had drinking cups before we had water in the house. Cows are demanding creatures. They support the family, and have soulful eyes and make mournful mooing noises that never let you forget who runs the show. In case you doubted, they could emphasize the point by suddenly arching their backs in the middle of milking and, for no earthly reason, roll you into the gutter with one foot in the milk pail, the cow's foot, not mine. I never knew that four legs could go in all directions, but they can, I was there. The mixture of milk and cow manure makes quite a paste to be decorated with. Mamma had come to the house, the first victim of a young heifer's resentment of human beggars stealing her milk. So

I—being the big-headed, proud, and educated beyond most of my rural friends who milked cows and forfeited higher education—I would take on the rowdy heifer! I wasn't scared. Mamma said, "Honey, be careful!"

"Never fear, Ma, I can handle her."

In a short time I returned to the house looking worse than Mamma had. Have you ever seen a cow's eyes when she's frightened? They get as big as silver dollars and they are like flashes of lightning that send electric shocks through their whole body, gyrating every nerve and muscle, and throwing it into action. We kept her and, eventually, she added to our support. Every cow had a name and a stanchion, and she responded to the name and found her own stanchion and would let no other have it. Now and then one would forget where her home was, or just have an ornery day and try for a change, but the home cow would never tolerate it.

10

Threshing time was always awe inspiring and exciting. The Hefter boys couldn't read or write but they had an inborn talent for machinery. Steam engines were taking over the then modern world. Threshing machines were steam powered. What an invention! No more threshing floors for the poets to write about. Fall came and grain stood neatly shocked in the field. A well-built shock of grain was a work of art. The grain was cut with a binder, so it was called a "grain binder," which it did. It cut the grain off at ground level and tied it in bundles of near equal size. Then the adults in the family put on heavy gloves and long sleeves of one kind or other, heavy to protect their arms, picked up a bundle of grain in each hand, leaned them against each other, then picked up another two. It was a definite procedure learned by practice, years of practice to become skilled. It was not for the weak or faint of heart. The shock was finished off with a bundle thrown on top as a roof to prevent the grain from being soaked in case of rain. Grains had to be dry when threshed.

Day breaks and we've been up for hours listening for the whistle of the steam engine. The teams are harnessed and hitched to hay wagons, wagons with wide racks mounted on them so as to carry large loads of hay or grain. Papa climbs the rack and takes up the reins and, without a nod, takes off for the sound of the whistle. This is the day they start at a neighbor's. Our kitchen is in high gear. The wood box is full of dry wood (or fairly dry; it was seldom a sure thing). Cutting wood for all the stoves was spare-time work and there was never enough spare time to have a pile drying for a year ahead. The cook stove in the kitchen was hot today. Pies are spreading their aroma beyond the open doors. The threshers will move to our house for dinner. They know the best cooks in the neighborhood and plan their moves strategically. Neighbor women drift in to help. There are potatoes to peel, stuffing to make, chicken to fry, a roast to prepare, gravy to make. Bread and rolls had been baked the previous day. Water needs to be pumped into buckets for drinking, and some in a milk can for cleaning up. The wash water, washbowl, soap, and towels are on a bench set up outside.

Dishes (big ones) for mashed potatoes, platters for meat, silverware. All the leaves had been put in the table—it will serve twelve at a time. How many are coming? Who knows—

fifteen? Twenty? These are hungry sweat-and-towel men. Coffee pots—big coffee pots, cold drinks, no ice of course, no refrigeration. All must be fresh today. Milk and cream from the water-filled tank. Amazing the talk that goes on as all the work gets done. This is a once-a-year neighborhood gathering. An amazing procedure. No burns, no cuts, no dishes broken. Laughter and chatter. Flies, oh, yes flies! Sticky strips hang from the ceiling, buzzing with flies dying from greed!

When the steam whistle blows it signals that they are finished on one job and can move to the next.

We kids watch, eager eyed, as the monster comes through the cut a quarter of a mile away, dragging its threshing machine behind it. It moves very slowly so the men with teams and wagons can come ahead. They park the wagons around the yard and unhitch the horses, water them at the water tank, feed them or tether them in a shady spot where they can munch on the grass. For the men, one dipper in the water pail serves all. They drink deeply, wash vigorously, splashing water on their hot, sweaty bodies wherever bare skin shows. Then they file into the dining room, and the passing of platters begin. The engineers are last. Locating the two machines properly takes time. The straw must blow out where the farmer wants the straw stack. The grain is stored in the grain bin in the hayloft. From there it comes down a chute to the main floor and is fed to the horses.

The operation is exciting to observe. One man mans the straw stack, shaping it properly. Two or more wagons haul the shocked grain from the fields and bring it to the barnyard and feed the noisy machine. The long, wide belt keeps the action going. The haulers time their loads so there's no idling of machinery.

It was a dangerous job for all involved—a no-nonsense type of duty. One careless move could bring total disaster, but I never heard of anyone getting injured. The belt itself was like a long dragon going round and round. If it broke it would wipe out anyone too near. The air was full of dust and chaff. All eyes were blurred and full of dust. But the engineers, self-trained men of talent, understood the giant they maintained. They knew the power of steam and how to harness it. Water, again, was a necessary element.

The gas engine in the Shanty lean-to worked that day too. The milk had to be kept cool in the small water tank, built of cement for that purpose and for extra needs in the house. The reservoir at the end of the wood range in the kitchen had to be kept full to supply hot water for the dinner cleanup. We always washed dishes in a metal dishpan, which we heated on the stove, along with a pan of water for rinsing. If you poked along at washing the dishes you might have to add more cold water. After I was "educated" I had trouble learning how to handle dishwashing without having heat to keep the water warm.

The men finished the job on our farm. The fields stood empty of shocks. The grain was good this year. The kernels were full and plump, no rust or disease. The oat bin was full. The stack was well formed, of course! Papa stacked it himself. It was the dirtiest job of all. The straw was blown through a big pipe that he maneuvered. The belt was run off the rolling shafts. The steam whistle blew, letting the next farm know, "We're on our way." None of the farms fed the threshers supper. When the job shut down, everyone either went home to their daily chores or to the next job they were asked to work. Everything was done on a labor-exchange basis. No one was paid. "You help me and I'll help you."

Now the kitchen help got a chance to eat, if there was anything left. After that, the cleanup. Those who could stay washed up the dishes, but by and large it was up to Mamma and the kids to straighten up, finish up, and put away. There were still eggs to gather, chickens to feed, and supper to get. Back to the barn to milk the cows after supper. Tomorrow was another day.

11

We sold milk now instead of cream. No more turning the separator to separate the cream. No more glorious sight of rich cream flowing from the short spout as we turned the separator crank at a designated speed…and no more rich, thick cream for the strawberries. So washing the separator and all its icky, yucky disks was a job gladly ended. We would run water through the separator at night and wash it after the morning separation. Horrors! What would the health nuts think of that today?

Mamma always hoped that her girls would have an easier life than she had, so she never asked us to wash the separator. Maybe it was because we wouldn't do it good enough. It was a nasty, slimy job. Our disks didn't have to be in numerical order as most did. That made the job a bit easier. Now we poured the milk through a strainer into ten-gallon milk cans instead of five-gallon ones, since we no longer had to lift the cans shoulder high to pour into the separator. By the time this change came I was lifting five-gallon cans of milk shoulder high and pouring the milk into the separator tank.

Hedwig and granddaughter with dairy utensils

Verneta was never hooked on barn work, she preferred housework. I preferred the barn! Even after Verneta married an Iowa farmer she never helped in the barn. Barn work was not for women! She was wise. She gave her husband Bill two sons but herself no daughters. One thing they had was water...spring water and a spring house where all commodities needing cooler temperatures could be stored.

No pumping and carrying. Iowa acreage was all under plow, no time wasted pulling stumps, cutting trees, picking rocks. If we had a five-acre field of hay, it was big! To Verneta it looked like a postage stamp on a 9 x 12 envelope.

And stones! After every rain, or at least once a year, we'd hitch a horse to the stone boat and pick up the big rocks that seemed to push up out of the ground and were too heavy to throw onto a wagon flatbed. Sometimes we made stone fences along the edge of the field. They had to be put somewhere, and no one in that age or location bought stones to decorate their yards. Some few built houses, and whenever I saw one I said, "I'm going to buy or build a stone house someday," but I never did.

Florence and Ruth, 1923

Papa was modern. He kept up with the times. He no longer cut hay with a scythe, except in rough places where the mower couldn't go. His horse-drawn mower had a sickle blade that was attached to the part he rode on, and he could raise it up and down as needed. It would cut a swath three feet wide! Around and around the field he went in glory. The ground was rough and it was really no joy ride, but it was a speedy way to cut hay. It lay neatly in swaths in thin layers. No hand raking in this age. The horse-drawn rake was a two-wheeled thing and wide. The wheels were large and between them were large curved teeth that dragged the hay along until the trip lever was pulled and the load was dropped. This was not done until the hay was dry. This was an automatic time of prayer for sunshine. Rain would rot and mold the hay and make it worthless.

Once the windrows of dry hay were raked the hay was thrown into small shocks with a pitchfork, manual labor, in the heat of summer. Hayracks were fastened onto wagons, the hay was pitched on. The shocks were placed so the wagon could go between and a man could be loading from both sides. The wagon driver distributed the hay so as to take a big load as well as keep the load from tipping over. The horses seemed to understand the process and mostly moved along without much driving. "Whoa" and "giddyap," except for turns, pretty well took care of that part. Unloading and forming hay stacks that would not get rain soaked and waste a lot of hay was another farm art. Papa's college education must have taught him how to learn fast or else his boyhood was spent on a farm.

Haystack. Probably Florence and Mildred Hefter Taubman

Farmers pray a lot even if it's not consciously. So much depends on the weather; actually, everything on the farm depends on the weather. They pray automatically for sunshine when the hay is cut but not yet in the barn loft or hay stack, and they pray for rain to end a drought. It has nothing to do with being in a church or what kind of a god they believe in. It has everything to do with being hungry. When farmers fail because crops fail, one automatically searches for a power great enough to control nature, and God is a mighty fine short name for that. Oh, God, let it rain! Or, oh God, don't let it rain.

12

Grandma and Grandpa Taubman's pictures hung on the wall, side by side, in Papa's and Mamma's bedroom. They were bust-size pictures in wide gilt frames. I never saw them in person, but still see their faces—old and stern, Grandpa bearded with a big lower lip, and Grandma with a little dust cap on her head. I never heard much about them except that Papa took Ruth once, in winter, by train back to Bryant, South Dakota. I suppose it was a time when Grandpa and Grandma were old, maybe dying. The train was very cold and Papa had to wrap little Ruth in his coonskin coat. That is as much as I remember hearing of Papa's home life. His parents were Germans from Germany, ten (I think) brothers who came over on the same boat. Ten Taubmans who never kept track of each other when they got off the boat in New York! In my ninety years I have not seen that name in print very often, accept for Papa's brother Charlie and his four sons. My brother had two sons, William and Larry, but Larry had four daughters. William had two sons. It is not a common name in the phone book.

Papa resisted the telephone until 1924 or '25 when Ruth and I were both in high school. Papa was great at keeping up to date but he had no time for small talk—there was work to do. Reading fiction was a waste of time. Verneta was a problem reader. Somehow she seemed to get story books from somewhere and would have her nose in a book which was *verboten.* There were lamps to fill with kerosene and chimneys to wash, bread to bake, clothes to wash in a tub with a washboard, and ironing to do on a board. Once, in the early days, we had a washing machine that was hand operated, an arm stood up and was activated by pulling and pushing on it. I recall it standing outside the Shanty one summer. Mostly we operated with two tubs, soap and washboard in one, rinse water in the other, and a boiler of water on the stove boiling the whites. In those days you had Sunday clothes and everyday work clothes. We wore an outfit to school clean on Monday and by Thursday, if necessary, an apron over it. Washing was done every two weeks. In winter by the end of two weeks a change of long underwear was like a gift from heaven. Children today are badly cheated. They have no opportunity to experience pure, undiluted, incomprehensible joy.

Oranges were an unheard of commodity in our house. Our fruit was strawberries from our strawberry bed—the fruit of our own sweat and blood. We plowed the land, we planted, and weeded, and nursed the plants along, and after a couple of years it gave us fruit, but fruit from other states? Shipped in? Never! So an orange in the Christmas stocking was surely from Santa! Some years Mamma canned a hundred quarts of strawberries and we had strawberry sauce all winter. To this day I don't get too carried away when strawberry season rolls around. I can pass up a piece of shortcake in June for a dish of ice cream, plain vanilla, with hot chocolate.

Now, ice cream we made in winter, a gallon at a time. We filled the gallon container with a mixture of milk, cream, eggs, sugar, and of course, vanilla, allowing for expansion as it froze. Put the container inside the larger container, pack it down with snow, or icicles, and coarse salt, fasten on the crank and start turning. If all went well we'd have ice cream in half an hour—or eventually. The dash was pulled out, laid on a plate, and everyone fought for a lick. It had to be promptly licked because homemade ice cream melts fast. A cork was put in the hole in the lid where the dash stuck out before and the whole freezer was packed with ice or snow until it was served—sometimes at a school event or for Sunday guests or just for the family on a holiday.

Some of the neighbors had sheds where they kept ice far into the summer. They went to the nearest lake after the ice was thick and, with long saws, cut large chunks, pulled the chunks out with ice tongs, brought them home on the sled, and stored them in the ice house, packing them with sawdust that had piled up while sawing wood for heat. And I think of these as "the good ol' days"? Life was so simple before the machine age arrived and work could be done swiftly and easily. The cushy, push-button life was on the way, however. Papa now had a tractor to pull stumps, a new big barn with more milk cows, and water in the barn. He rented some acres of sandy soil and planted potatoes. He rented hay land also, and hauled the hay home and put it in the barn loft.

Papa went to sales, and one day he came home with a fancy two-piece organ. The top section came off. It was of beautifully carved wood with a mirror set in and shelves for flowers or a lamp to sit on. Usually he came home with machinery or ten bushels of black popcorn on the cob that was stored on the upstairs screened porch. It lasted us for years and was a feast for the long winter evenings. As to the organ and the initial excitement, Ruth and I soon learned it was not the greatest idea Papa (or Mamma?) ever had. We began taking lessons from a neighbor lady—a family friend. Lessons cost fifty cents each for a half hour. We weren't the greatest material. We soon hated to practice, and Mamma was too busy to apply the necessary force. It got the best workout on the occasions when the furniture was pushed back and one of the neighbors who played by ear volunteered to accompany old man Siger on his fiddle. When I had to take music in college, and had to learn to play "Three Blind

Mice" I was thankful for what little I did know and spent the rest of my teaching career wishing Mamma had had time to stand over me at the organ with a hickory stick. It would have simplified teaching small children. That was one of two mistakes I made "in the beginning." The second biggie was not listening to my big and wise sister who told me to take Latin so I would understand English grammar. That may have helped me in developing my desire to become a writer.

13

So I entered high school in 1923 a very timid soul. I can't recall how Ruth got to school the year before. She was the weak one who was sheltered more than the rest of us. However, we were raised almost as twins, we shared a room and a bed and our secrets. My eighth grade in rural school, and her first year of town school, should be a memorable era; strange, I cannot recall the circumstances that year.

When I began high school Ruth and I rode to school with the grandson of a neighbor who could drive a car. When winter weather set in, Papa made arrangements with the Olsons, who also had two daughters going on to high school, to rent the upstairs of a private home in town where four of us would stay, doing light housekeeping. Our driver got a room in someone else's upstairs. We went home on Friday after school and, on Sunday night, each family got their kids to town by horse-drawn vehicles loaded with food for a week.

Living with our friends was a real test of friendship, but we made it 'till spring when we could travel home daily. Two things I recall. One, our driver visited us once and for entertainment we sat on five straight chairs (there were no other kind) and threw a light bulb about for entertainment. We were still in the age of innocence. The second was when the siren, which stood next to our house, went off in the middle of the night. We had never heard a siren, and it practically blew us out of bed. The family downstairs told us there was a fire downtown. The Mercantile, the town's one large all-purpose store, was burning. This was winter, of course, since we were living in town, and the store was only a block or two away. We jumped into some clothes and took off for Main Street. It was a big fire and all the town and volunteer fire department were out. Flames shot into the sky. There was no stopping it. Shivering with excitement as well as cold, even though the heat was terrific, we watched the disaster of the year.

Spring came and we took to the road again. One afternoon, as we were traveling across a stretch of road that was built up above four-foot banks, the wishbone of the car that controlled the front wheels came loose and the car made a sharp left turn and went nose down into the ditch. I suppose we were traveling at least thirty-five miles per hour. So there we sat on end, not knowing how we got there. We were only a mile or so from home—our home—and we walked there. Telephones had invaded our area and, of course, everyone with kids in school almost had to have one. The lines were busy that afternoon.

We had the wall phone that had a crank on the side. Our ring was a long and three shorts. Everyone on the line would hear all rings. Interest was high, and everyone listened in, sometimes so many that you'd have to say, "Will everybody please hang up? This is a call from 'so-and-so,' and I can't get the message."

One fall, when I was the only one in high school, Pa had offered, or was asked, to board someone's pony with the understanding that I was to exercise it by riding back and forth to school. Winter came late that year, so I was able to ride well into the school season. Days were short, it got dark early. I stayed after school one day to work on something. When I came out it was dusk. The stable where I kept the horse was locked! I found a phone somewhere, the switchboard operator was probably still on duty, and called home. Mamma said, "Pete is probably in the tavern. You'll have to go down there and find him." I think I was a junior that year and Ruth missed half a year due to poor health. Go to the tavern! My mom was telling me to go in a tavern! I was even too shy to go into the soda fountain. But I had no choice. I had to take the horse home, and he had to take me home! With knocking knees I opened the tavern door, and there was Pete. He knew my problem and, without words, we walked to the stable and I got my pony.

One afternoon—maybe it was the same day—we were loping along the same grade where the car had gone over, and I got thrown. There had been a light snow, and it was dark. The road was white until we got halfway across the grade where the wind had swept a small area bare. The pony was loping along just fine, and my mind was doing whatever a mind does when you're riding a horse—daydreaming? So I wasn't prepared for a sudden stop, which is what happened when the pony's feet hit the edge of bare land. He stopped abruptly, and I kept going. I still had the reins in my hand but I was out front instead of on top. It was a quick jolt into reality. The pony never moved. I picked myself up and looked at him. He was as scared as I was. I couldn't find the courage to try and mount. Like with the car incident, I was a mile from home. I started to lead and the pony decided if the black road was safe for me it was safe for him, and we walked on together quite peaceably. As I neared the turn into our farm I had to do something. No way could I walk to the house leading that pony. No way! Lawrence would never let me live it down. I mounted. I can't remember if my fall was a secret until now or not. I was never teased, so it must have been.

Lawrence was a surrogate father to me. Papa was too busy by the time I came along, but Lawrence favored me and spoiled me. Verneta and Lawrence fought. Ruth was not strong, so I was his favorite. There was no demonstrative love or affection in our family. "Honey" was just a handle I inherited to distinguish me from Lawrence, who had insisted that I be named "Florence." I was Honey when I was in trouble, as well as when I was told to carry in wood.

14

The wood box was always empty, it seemed. It was built on the outside of the house, with a latched door that opened into the house, so we could get the wood we needed for the stove. To fill it you had to lift off the little outside roof cover and set it aside.

Lawrence's children: Lorraine, Beverlee, and Larry; Verneta's children: Frank and Jere in front of the woodbox

The wood was usually in a heap at the end of the Shanty across the driveway. Our driveway was U-shaped, coming up the south side of the house and out the north side. So Ruth and I carried armloads across the driveway, mounted two steps and dumped the wood into the box. Mamma liked it if we put it in straight. The box was as wide as a stick of firewood for the kitchen range. It held a lot if you stood on your head and straightened it out. You also had to kind of stand on your head in the wood box to reach the wood in the bottom from the inside. Our wood never had a chance to dry out. It was lucky to get cut and thrown in the pile. The pile was never neatly stacked. There was never time. By the time the timber was cut in the woods, hauled home and sawed with a circular motor-powered saw, and thrown in a heap, it was time to clean barns, feed chickens, milk cows, fix a harness, clean a chicken coop, or whatever. "Idle hands are the devil's workshop," and at our house there was no devil's workshop. So we filled the wood box and put the lid back on. It was a neat idea. It beat carrying the wood in through the kitchen door and dumping it in a box. Beat tracking up the wood floor in the kitchen and letting in flies in summer. Mamma had the oven full of wet green wood a lot of the time, trying to dry it out a little.

The Wood Pile Under Snow: Florence and Ruth

Every day, especially in winter, there were ashes to carry out and dump somewhere, like the bucket of dirty water—get it away from the house. One summer evening, as darkness fell, Pa and Ma and I each took a can of kerosene and went out to the clearing where all the small branches were put in neat piles after cutting and trimming them off the trees. The trees were our firewood. The piles of branches had dried and were ready for burning. We hurried along, each choosing a different pile, splashed some kerosene on and threw in a lighted wooden match. It was wind still and beautiful out. Night fell. The air was full of the sweet odor of burning brush. The field was alight like no Roman Empire. It was a glorious evening. We stood about in the silence, broken only by the crackling fire, and watched as the piles turned to ashes and it was safe to leave. Then we went home, carrying with us the smell of wood smoke on our clothing.

The neighbor's fence line to the west bordered our land just across the driveway. A few acres of second growth timber separated our buildings. In the spring, Ruth and I competed to see who would be the first to find a mayflower—white lilies with three leaves that grew profusely in their woodlot along their fence line—and we picked trilliums. (Fences were to keep cows out, not children.)

Once when I was eleven or twelve, and Pa had potatoes planted on the rented sandy soil, we girls, with buckets in hand, followed the horse-drawn potato picking machine and gathered potatoes the machine kicked out. The machine dug under and brought up potatoes, dirt and all, and ran them over a moving grate. The dirt fell through and the potatoes rode to the end and fell off. Harvest time was late fall. The weather was announcing the coming of winter. It was time to harvest and all hands (able hands) were needed. Pa paid us a few cents per bucketful. He had a chart attached to the wagon where we kept score. The potatoes were dumped down a chute into a bin in the basement. The basement had stone and cement walls, but a dirt floor. Potatoes would keep 'till next harvest. Many were cooked in the "witches brew" kettle out near the hog pen, along with all the table scraps, or whatever, and fed to the pigs. The pigs probably had a hot stew that would really bring the Prodigal Son, who wasted his inheritance, home to his father's house.

But, as for me, I earned between five and six dollars and spent a glorious fall studying the Sears & Roebuck catalog, deciding which pair of shoes to buy. It took days to decide. At last I sent the order and waited impatiently for the mailman to leave a box on the wheel where our mailbox was attached. Such anxiety, such eager waiting! I was hard on shoes. I ran them over. I went through the soles. Papa, having been in the harness business in South Dakota, was able to work with leather in its various uses. He had two sizes of lasts and could do big and smaller shoes. We didn't know about shoe repair shops. This was evening work for Papa. He could sit down and be busy. Idle hands..., you know. The mail came through come rain, snow, or hail. The brown shoes that laced up well above the ankle arrived. They were beautiful. Never before, or since, have I had a pair to equal them. They were to be saved for special occasions, until my present footwear was irreparable or I outgrew them. Then one night when the west wind was blowing in our direction our neighbor's timber caught fire. The fire was racing our way. Mamma and Papa got us up in the middle of the night to be ready. We dressed and I set my new shoes at the head of the stairs so if it came through and burned our house I would have one precious thing—my new shoes, bought with my own money! The fire died out and my shoes were safe. The trilliums blossomed more profusely than ever the next spring. Violets grew in abundance everywhere and Ruth beat me again, finding the first mayflower. Dandelions grew best of all. We picked their heads off and Ma made wine out of them. Social drinking was not our lifestyle, but Papa had to have a shot of brandy to open his eyes at 4:30 or 5:00 A.M. to get his day started and maintain strength 'till barn chores, milking, feeding, etc., was done and he could come to the house and replenish his bodily food with long-cooked oatmeal, pancakes, fried potatoes, and bacon. That would carry him 'till noon. Coffee breaks were not a part of his schedule.

15

TB and Career Choices

I am beginning to realize as I write what a dominating part TB played in my life and that of the entire family, from my high school days to Ruth's marriage.

There was the back porch that had to be screened, the front porch added on, the years of visiting Ruth in all the sanitariums in Wisconsin—Hawthorne, near Superior, two different ones in Eau Claire, and the Lutheran Wheatridge in Denver Colorado. We almost lost her in Hawthorne where the institution had a beautiful large dairy herd. The cure for TB was bed rest and good food. The beautiful herd tested out positive for Bang's disease (undulant fever). They lost the entire herd. Years later, after Ruth was married, a blood sample was positive for undulant fever and a state officer from Madison showed up at her Shell Lake home asking where she was getting raw milk. That dated back to those days in Hawthorne. Undulant fever and TB have similar symptoms and was, no doubt, the cause of her going downhill while at Hawthorne.

Milk was not pasteurized in those days. When cattle were found to have Bangs disease, which causes undulant fever in humans, they were slaughtered

At one point when it seemed evident that recovery was not for her, and she was so weak we had to hold her up, we decided we might as well take her out for a weekend and give her a change of atmosphere. Dad, Mom and I rented a cabin in the woods and, for once, spent a holiday together away from home, the only one in my lifetime. It was not a joyous vacation but we tried to be happy together. Then for years after she began to recover she was out a year and then back into another sanitarium—in and out.

Ruth and Frank, the weekend outing, 1933

Hedwig and Ruth, the weekend outing, 1933

Ruth and Hedwig, the weekend outing, 1933

Our TB problem caused me to skip five years of my life—from college graduation to my devious plans to establish in Colorado. Actually, I'll go back to how my second year in college got funded. Verneta was married by now and had fulfilled her obligation (?) to fund me. I never worried about how that would happen. I never considered taking a summer job. I either was needed on the farm or just had a mental block. Verneta was always out of the home. I was always back home. In any case, Mamma's Papa died and left her a little money. She loaned me $100 for my second year, which I almost blew by nearly flunking grammar. By the skin of my teeth I graduated.

Florence on campus

The college car took a load of us out to Withee, some forty miles from Eau Claire, where we applied for job openings. This was May 1930. Two of the group got jobs and one of them was me! Only seven of our class of about forty got jobs. The depression was on. No money, no jobs. The rich who lost everything were jumping off house tops, and the poor were still poor, as usual. I taught first and second grades for three years in Withee, a Danish community. Counting students in the class pictures I have, I must have had about thirty-six pupils. Wages were lowered every spring with new contracts. The third year we were paid in scrip, which was non-negotiable. IOUs, actually.

I was as stupid about teaching as a youth can be. I assumed I could carry on somehow as the student teachers did in college. The third and fourth grade teacher was an old-timer and a local woman. Just before bell time the first day she walked into my room and said, "What system of reading are you planning to use?" System? I was going to teach colors, numbers, how to tie their shoes, count to 100, and the first week the first graders had to learn to get along without Mamma. Second grade would go on their own, I guess. College had really not prepared me for actual classroom situations. The third and fourth grade teacher was not happy with a greenhorn, had little love for me, and kept an eagle eye on my methods. I had no great love for her either. I surely needed her, but we were never bosom pals! She showed me where the textbooks were that first day. They were on the lower level where the coats, boots, and buckets were left. Dick and Jane and Spot were all there. I shudder now at my ignorance and the fact that there had been no preschool faculty meeting. Or had I not arrived in time?

I was told by someone to get a room at the jewelry house where all teachers boarded. The master of the house had a jewelry shop in front. The upstairs had a heated living room and one bath. One heated bedroom was occupied by a very sedate, longtime, maiden lady who taught seventh and eighth grades. Two high school teachers had a couple of unheated rooms and the other new teacher that applied with me (known as "Sis") and I had the frosty bedroom and the down quilt. Momma Nelson ruled the roost with an iron hand and knew everybody's business all over town. Papa Nelson was quiet and pleasant and fit well with his fine jewelry. The first thing I didn't do right was drink coffee for breakfast.

My second year I moved in with a private family, the Hansens. I had their son in first grade. Grandpa lived with them and he was a jolly old Dane.

The Hansen family

As I said, Withee was a Danish community and Grandpa went about the house singing Danish tunes. The Hansens were a wonderful couple and home life was a happy life. They ran a grocery store. I was very happy there.

At the end of my second year I bought a Model A Ford from my friend Emma, the math teacher. She had bought it new for $600. It was a sedan, enclosed with glass windows! It had a starter and heater! First class, wow! I had ridden in it just about every mile it had traveled. She pampered that car and had it in the garage for every little thing. It was like new and I bought it for $300. Then Emma found me a summer job working for some lakeshore people spending the summer in the woods. I gave the Model A to my folks so they could have transportation to go see Ruth.

Florence and the Model A

I made a lousy maid, or else I had a very poor boss. Some people have the gift of walking into anyone's kitchen and taking over. I had no such talents. I had to be told to wash windows and cook, etc. I had a closet for a bedroom. I couldn't seem to fit. I stayed on 'till I had a little money, and went home. How was I different from the twenty-first century generation? Not much. I left my car with Dad who said, "Maybe buying it was as good an idea as any." Who knew what to do in this Depression?

While Emma still owned the car she found a farmer and married him. I lost my job at the end of my third year, just when I was comfortable and so conceited I thought I was indispensable

In the spring, rumors were going around that Miss Taubman was not being rehired. Contracts were out. I finally went to the grocery store and confronted a board member who was manager, or part owner, with my landlord, Hansen. "Oh," he said, "didn't anyone tell you? The banker's daughter graduated from Eau Claire and, jobs being scarce, they gave your job to her." My top blew off! I wasn't raised in a barn for nothin', and I wasn't the pampered baby of the family for nothin'. I have *no* idea what I said, I only remember my rage and how I stormed and cried. I had given them the best years of my life, etc. That much of the storm I remember still at age ninety. I was then nineteen or twenty years old. Somehow, the board made good the three months of scrip at the end of the year, and a load of us piled into somebody's car and went to Minneapolis, stayed in a hotel, and shopped. My first really big-city stuff. I bought a gorgeous red coat with a black fur collar. Gosh, it was beautiful. I got caught in the rain wearing it later and the black ran onto the red. It was a heartbreak.

Florence and coat, with friend

16

Another crushing blow to my pride in my first year of having an income occurred after a trip to Eau Claire—big trip—to the millinery shop. Hundreds of hats. A woman's heyday. First one style, then another; primp and pose in front of and between the many mirrors. It was a first for me. At last I settled on just the one. It was a grosgrain ribbon one, lavender color. It sort of wound around the head and had a large ostrich plume attached to the right side that hung down my cheek. It was simply beautiful. I loved it. Most hats were $1.98, but this one was $7.00! I bought it! That night I put it on to model my prize for the envious group in the living room upstairs. Well, our oldest and most sophisticated member— the quiet, proper, dignified member of the group—burst out laughing. "Are you going to a circus?" she asked. I suppose I resembled Greta Garbo, but the rest of my wardrobe... Well,

I was mortally wounded. The hat was an instant curse. I was a "waste not want not" character—like the Red Cross shoes I *had* to wear since I couldn't replace them. No way could I be comfortable in the hat, but I couldn't just throw it away! No way! Neither could I wear it with my red and green plaid Chippewa jacket. I removed the feather and dyed it black. Two of the teachers and I took a trip east to Washington D.C. in my car.

Florence at the Chicago World's Fair, 1933; National Geographic exhibit relocated to background

While crossing the Potomac River, with the windows open, the hat blew out of a back window and into the river. It was a good solution to a problem I couldn't handle. Some learnin' comes awful, hard and it's usually the simple lessons. I was pretty spiteful to the teacher who caused my dilemma. I attacked her religion. She was Catholic. Years later, when I became a convert, I was horrified at my long-past unholy conduct and I apologized by mail. I never knew if she received it, but it never returned. She may have been dead by that time. I only hope God has forgiven me! I had no religion at that time.

Now I was jobless, and hatless, and immature. I was still a farm girl accustomed to dealing with cattle, and quiet, and peace. It was people who were the problem! I was frank, honest, and tactless, but somehow, despite it all, I seemed to land on my feet. I got a job in the next town, Curtiss, Wisconsin. Curtiss was only a wide place in the road, with a cheese factory—Colby cheese—to support it. It had a three-room school with a principal who taught grades seven and eight, an intermediate taught grades four, five, and six, and me with grades one, two, and three, a demotion for me but a job. I was now under county supervision.

My lessons in dealing with people met a new low. In Withee we had state supervision, but now the county supervisor tagged silently along. She remembered me, and they were not good memories. It seems I had a bad habit of defending my college-taught methods, which I later realized were not always practical and needed to be adjusted to the circumstance.

I liked the state supervisor. I suppose she was tolerant of my youthful ignorance. She was kind, though critical. But the county supervisor was clearly not impressed—or was over-impressed with my *frankness*. Our school *Annual* had one remark following my name: "*Frank* Taubman," my father's name. Why did it follow my name? I was naïve besides. I didn't remember her—which was bad. But she *did* remember me. I could do nothing right. And her criticism had nothing to do with how or what the children were learning. If I had them stand to recite, that was wrong. If I let them sit, that was improper. There was nothing helpful in her report. For two years this went on. I became a nervous wreck. I went home that second summer feeling, as we now say in 2001, burnt out! I spent the summer resting at home, my parents now lived in a rented house, and Lawrence ran the farm.

17

Colorado Bound

Maybe it was time for me to check my own health status. I was always a TB risk, having spent my life sleeping with Ruth, and being like a twin sister. In those days, you didn't go to the doctor and get checked up once a year. You just went if you were sick in bed, or he came to see you when you were sick in bed. I didn't want to be another family victim of TB, so I decided to go and have a checkup. The advice was, as long as I had the insurance, take advantage of it and get out to Woodmen's. I sent my teaching contract back unsigned when I found that Woodmen Insurance would take me to Colorado. It was actually sort of a scheme of mine.

After riding a Greyhound bus for three days and two nights, Superintendent John E. Swanger, I believe his name was, met me in Colorado Springs and drove me about fifteen miles to Woodmen TB Village. He was a jolly person and made me feel very much at home, like I was wanted and would be safe with them. I enjoyed the mountain ride, it was my first experience in mountains. We got to the sanitarium in the evening. I don't recall any particular details about checking in. I was no doubt exhausted.

Woodmen was a beautiful campus, and was a great TB facility for men. It had everything, like a small village. When the men reached a certain point of recovery they lived in individual huts—probably over a hundred. At that time Woodmen was not really prepared to accommodate women. The women stayed in the big hospital and no outdoor provisions had been made. The main hospital backed into the mountain with only space enough for a car to drive around it. Nine rooms on the first floor served the women, but I was number ten, so I was put on the second floor— with the men—in a large private room in the back corner. My window looked out at the big rock wall of the mountain. It was the only room on that side, sort of separated from the rows of doors. My main door opened onto the hall, but I had a side door opposite the rock wall that opened onto the stairway.

I was thin and ran a temperature and had a family history of TB. That was enough to keep me there for eleven months. My aim was still to live in Colorado and get Ruth out there. One of my memories was a doctor, whose name I can't remember, but he was tall and thin, with shaggy white hair.

I didn't know if he was going to eat me up or smile. Well, he smiled. And when he smiled, all the ice broke. He looked at my name, which I had signed Florence M.M. Taubman (I was named after my mother's and father's sisters—one was Mary and the other was Marie, so I was named Florence Mary Marie). At that time Mickey Mouse was pretty popular, and the doctor looked at my signature and said, "M.M. I suppose that means Mickey Mouse." Well, I never signed it that way again, believe me. But it was a good joke.

I was put to bed and was supposed to stay there. This was the cure in those days. I had my meals in bed. I must have had bed baths, I can't remember any more. I suppose I went through the usual x-rays and that sort of thing. I never had an active sputum, but I had a temperature, which nobody around there liked. It wasn't much, but it was enough to be annoying and threaten me with TB ahead. I tried to entertain myself, but mostly I was climbing the walls. I had a potty in my closet, but sometimes I'd sneak down the stairs to the girls' bathroom. The few women were from all different states and all different ages. Our youngest was a fourteen- or fifteen-year-old. It was full of girl talk down there. I was never caught sneaking downstairs, but I wonder now if perhaps that was intentional.

We bleached hair, did girl talk, and had a great time in that bathroom. Sadly, I thought bleached blondes were better—"Blondes have more fun" was the popular slogan so I allowed one of the girls, who encouraged me, to bleach my hair. That was a mistake. When I washed it, it tangled so terribly I couldn't get a comb through it. So I got a home perm, and that was worse yet. Eventually, all my hair broke off about an inch from my head. That was the end of my desire to be a blonde. I have just accepted my weak, colorless hair to this day.

So they kept me there for eleven months. No, I wasn't in bed all the time. They let me out of bed to join in some activities. I got to go to a few movies and met a few guys and all that good stuff, but there wasn't a lot of mingling. Of course we patients were taken on rides. We saw the Garden of Gods, and I was getting pretty much attached to Colorado. I really loved it. I decided I would make an effort to stay out there and get my tubercular sister to this better climate. Maybe that would help her.

I did a lot of writing, tried out poetry in an effort to see if I had any talent at all. My friends back home kept writing and encouraging me, one of them even came all the way out there to see me, and took me down to Colorado Springs where we stayed overnight in a motel. The next day we went to Pikes Peak. We really enjoyed that day together. We were all so poor back then that money really had value. Her parents, who didn't want either of them to know, had each given her $5, and told her, "You and Florence have a good time." We felt pretty rich and pretty much loved. We had parents who really cared, and it was one of the nicest things I had happen.

18

Dodson was a bleached blonde about my age and we became good friends. She's the one who bleached my hair. My stubble provided entertainment enough for quite some time. While we bleached and fussed with hair I learned the story of a bad marriage to a man who was still trying to get her back. She was a very smart businesswoman and left Woodmen a couple of months ahead of me, went to Denver, got a good job, and set up in an apartment. Later she helped me get out and get started again in Colorado. I lived with her, clerked in the lingerie department on the third or fourth floor at the May Company Department Store downtown. I don't know that I made a great sales lady, but I learned a lot and my vision of life expanded considerably. Without a car—since I gave mine to my dad—I walked to and from the May Company. The depression was on, especially for me. Being poor in the country on a farm was one thing, with Ma and Pa still providing food for the table. Being poor in a big city—well, another story indeed. I had never lived the apartment life.

My clerking job did not feed me and pay my share of the rent, even though I walked to work and was a scrupulous spender. I applied for a job at Sears that paid more, but it was advertising hosiery by walking in the front window—only my legs would show. No one would see to whom they belonged. I wasn't sure this would be morally correct. What would Mamma say? But I needn't worry. I failed the test. The legs passed but the clumsy walk didn't.

I was still hungry and down to my last quarter—literally! As I walked down the street a sign hanging from a storefront was shaped like a huge frosty milkshake. A quarter would buy one! I went in. It was a Depression milkshake, thick with something, but not even cold. They forgot the ice cream. Whatever it was, I drank it, it was something in my stomach. I went home penniless 'till payday.

I visited the Rocky Mountain Teachers Placement Agency to enquire about teaching jobs. My aim was to get established and bring Ruth out. They called me one day in March and said, "There's a job opening in Kiowa, Colorado, a little town on the prairie, fifty miles east of Denver." But—and that was a big but—they couldn't recommend me because Colorado was overrun with TB patients from all over. My history would kill the possibilities even though I had never had a positive sputum test. But, in today's language, they said, "Go for it, good luck." It was a March opening of grades one and two—right down my alley, and they were desperate. The teacher was about to have a baby and the vacancy had to be filled. I had walked miles and miles and knew Denver by heart. I had even tried selling insurance door to door, but now where in the world was Kiowa?

It was 1936. Rain—or lack of it for three years—had led to crop failures. (Papa lost his farm due to the Depression and to years of consecutive crop failure—an old, broken, and poverty-stricken man.) The earth was shifting and Texas soil was moving into Colorado. The air was full of it. Some days one could hardly see for sand shifting. And I was trying to find Kiowa. It was somewhere out of my reach. There were no trains or busses to it. I could find no transportation. My roommate said, "There's got to be! They have to have milk and other things delivered." And she found it—a Star Mail Route that could take passengers. It went to Kiowa. We got that arranged and I did get to Kiowa, stopping here and there along the way.

19

Kiowa was a typical little prairie town. The board met with me and we got along just fine, but they had not received my credentials from the Rocky Mountain Teachers Placement Agency. As soon as they came, I'd be hired. So I had to start talking my way out of a possible problem again. I knew my TB history, and the fact that I had been in the sanitarium, would be in the report and would cause a final NO. I had never coughed or had actual "live bugs," as we used to refer to them. I had symptoms and history that was condemning. I had no fear of spreading the disease. Diplomacy was not my forte, but hunger can make drastic changes. Three board members were there. I must have said something right or the men were hungry and anxious to get home. Anyway one of them said, "Hey, I've got to milk cows. Let's forget the agency's recommendation and hire her." They had to have a teacher to finish out the year. It was March, and I signed the contract! Wow! What a victorious day.

Kiowa had a larger school on the hill that housed grades five through twelve, but due to an overflow of pupils the little old two-room building right downtown was put back into use for grades one through four. Two of us were teaching in the little school. We had no supervision. We had our own way about everything, and we had our own playground. Nobody bothered us; no big kids harassed us. It was simply a perfect setup. From my window I could see Pikes Peak on a clear day. The wind blew and the windows rattled. Sand piled up on the sills overnight. Three years of no rain. Farmers were desperate, the economy was worse. But we were all in it together and those western ranchers could handle it. No one talked about it. We had a day to live, and we lived it.

The third and fourth grade teacher was an older widow lady. She had a boyfriend from Denver and a big bowser of a dog. She was quite dignified and lived in the hotel. We got along just fine.

I was boarding with a great family of three—a couple and their teenage daughter. They were already boarding two teachers in their bungalow, but they cleaned out an oversized closet and took me in. They also boarded a Pekinese dog— yippy little cuss whom I detested. He met me at the door in all his fury. I wanted to kick him over the moon, but he was too close to the ground and too quick for me. He was Casey's dog (the eighteen-year-old) and she would have deported me to the moon had I succeeded. I was treated like family, and they laughed at my dog frustrations.

Papa Bud and daughter Casey were the greatest companions—crazy people together—and Mamma Jessie wasn't far behind. The teachers from the school on the hill had little to do with us four. The family took me to the Saturday night dance in the town hall the first weekend I moved in. Dancing was a family affair. No baby sitters. You brought the kids along. You didn't live if you didn't dance. Bud was a tall, well-built westerner, hat and all, and of course he had to have a dance with the new teacher. He was a powerful dancer and there was no question about who was leading. My feet barely touched the ground. As we were speeding around the hall, Bud stepped on a marble! He went down like a ton of bricks, flat on his back. Guess where I was? And I hadn't even taught my first day!

It was a delightful two years in Kiowa. The big school didn't seem to know we existed, which was wonderful.

Later, after finishing out that year and returning for my first full year, I sent for Ruth. She was out of the sanitarium again and able to come. I used the family sewing machine and sewed my own clothes and Ruth's. We fixed crude living quarters in the basement behind the furnace. We weren't down there a lot, we were with the family (and dog!). They loved Ruth and showed her a good time. She dated Jessie's brother.

The air was great even though dust piled up over the fences, which were full of tumbleweeds. But there were few fences. In my class were Texas children sent to Kiowa because of the dust storms in Texas. It blew from Texas to Colorado. We went to Denver often—fifty miles to these ranchers was like across the street. We took trips to the mountains, skied on the foothills. I couldn't make it up to where the ski tow began. Berthoud Pass, Georgetown—all new experiences for us. No one had any money, but we had a lot of fun.

Florence, 1938

One Easter morning we drove to the Red Rock Natural Amphitheater near Colorado Springs to attend sunrise services. We didn't wear Easter bonnets. It was a beautiful sunrise, very cold. It was a once-in-a-lifetime experience. Casey and her boyfriend were often with us and usually double-dated with Jessie and Bud. They didn't approve of the boyfriend, but they tolerated him. I don't think he was overly ambitious then, but years later, when I returned, Casey was married and had raised a couple of children and was home dying of cancer. She looked great, and her attitude was still optimistic.

20

Summers, as always, caught me broke. Mrs. Simon, teacher of grades three and four, one day said, "Florence, let's go up in the mountains. There's a job up there we can do in the summertime." She would only take it if I would join her. Halfway up the mountain between Denver and Central City was a lonely gas stop, restaurant, and dance hall combination. Cars usually vapor-locked by the time they got that high and came limping in for help, sometimes bringing us business. The cure for vapor lock at that time was to sit and wait a half hour, then proceed until the next time it happened.

Simon and I, and the dog, took the job for the summer. It was the front door to a nudist camp in the mountains behind it. The owner of the stop and the camp was a gaunt, rawboned man, neither friendly nor unfriendly, who wore a shirt and overalls when he came down from camp.

Denver—or Colorado—laws forbade nudist camps and tried to shut them down. Nudism was a family affair! When they appeared in court they wore their fine furs and expensive clothes. (Maybe nudism was an outgrowth of the TB cure of sunbathing on the sanitarium roof for which Colorado was famous.)

My parents and the Proberts drove out in August 1938. Jere was a baby and Verneta was sick all the way, surviving on 7-Up. Any trip brought on this condition, but she survived it. Our boss put them up in one of the cabins in the woods. I don't think they saw much, but I don't think they slept much either.

I thought Central City was the most exciting place I'd ever seen. The streets to the entrance of the theaters and hotels were paved with gold brick when celebrities arrived. At the tavern the "face on the barroom floor" still appeared. A real face of a real woman of extreme wealth who died in extreme poverty. To my uneducated, un-historic mentality, it was fantastic, beyond belief. So while our patrons waited for their cars to cool I filled their gas tanks, washed their windshields, and regaled them with the wonders of Central City.

Florence

One customer remarked, "Gee, we couldn't find anyone to tell us what to see in Central City." I replied, "You talked to natives; they've lived with its splendor and take it for granted. I'm a native of Wisconsin. It's all new and unbelievable to me."

Saturday nights the ceiling over the station bounced, the music blared, and the natives danced in the hall overhead. At midnight we served hamburgers and coffee and whatever else the boss in his overalls furnished for sale. After we got to bed in the back room and to sleep, sometimes our watchdog would bark. Was it a prowler? Or an animal he was barking at? No problem. Morning came and we were still there, unharmed.

Once the boss came down to take gas to a car a mile down the hill. I guess we had a telephone connection but I don't remember using one. Anyway, for some unremembered reason, I rode along to deliver the gas. It was a breathtaking experience. Mr. Boss suddenly turned around in the middle of the road on a curve with a stone wall on the left and a drop into eternity on the right. The road was barely two lanes wide, so he inched forward and back until we were finally turned around. I was so terrified I can remember nothing else about that gas delivery. I never went again!

Our only company that we could call friends was an interesting couple who lived nearby. He was rather small and friendly, and about the homeliest little cowboy I've seen. Not a young man, perhaps middle aged. His face was weathered like his cowboy hat. She was a young, beautiful lady who rode the saddle very well. She also beautified the little red, top-down sports car they rode around in. They were not part of the nudist colony. They took us beer drinking once to a place where the mugs held a quart or maybe more. Anyway, riding home in the rumble seat just above the exhaust was not a good idea, but where else? Those kind people didn't bring the car down next day for me to clean. Good thing, since I wasn't seeing too good. My head was on malfunction.

Two things happened before we finished our summer job. While my parents and my sister, the Proberts, were there they took me back to Kiowa to say my farewells and close my bank account. They dropped me off in Denver and started their trip back to Wisconsin. I went into a drug store to make a call from the telephone booth. I have never been a fainting person, but that day I was blacking out in the booth. I staggered to the soda fountain and tried to yell for water, but it seemed no one heard me. Finally someone noticed I was in trouble and gave me water. I was picked up and went home. Then I discovered I had no purse. My year's savings, probably $50, was gone and again I was batting zero. The purse was not in the phone booth. There was no recovery.

The teachers' agency found me another job to apply for on the other side of the mountain in the Steamboat Springs area. It was a little town called Phippsburg, a small settlement of miners' families, with a store, a grade school, and Baptist church. It was a town where all languages could be heard on the streets. That's when disaster number two happened. I had to go to Phippsburg for my first day of school. Ordinarily I would be able to take the Moffat train that passed through many tunnels from Denver, one ten miles long; however, the rains came and washed out the tracks to Phippsburg. That meant the Moffat train was inoperable. There were no buses or any other transportation available, and it was a long hike over two mountain passes. I *had* to be there, and I was quite overcome with this tragedy. Final act, Simon and the boyfriend took me. I arrived in time for the first day of school and the board couldn't believe it. They were used to the Moffat Line getting washed out. They hadn't contacted me by phone and had hired a substitute, so nobody was concerned, except me. They accepted that the Moffat would go out once or more a year and they just handled it. They had a substitute ready to step in and hold the fort until the tracks were fixed.

I moved into a little two-room log cabin they had arranged for me to live in. One big living room held two daybeds for sleeping on and a little Toonerville Trolley-type stove. (I don't suppose any of you remember the Toonerville Trolley comics. It was a one-picture deal with a little stove that danced around.) This one danced around when it got too hot, and it got red hot in a hurry. However, it didn't stay that way long. There was a lean-to across the back that was the kitchen-dining room. We had a water pail, a pump, and a path. When the snow started to thaw, the water would run down the mountain and under the door into the kitchen. When we got up in the morning the kitchen floor would be like a skating rink, but we'd heat up that little old stove and it soon warmed up. Josephine, the teacher who taught grades three and four, shared the cabin with me. Another, older, woman had fifth and sixth grades, and the principal—I think his name was Mr. Seller—had seventh and eighth. He was a young unmarried man. I got the job and was happy to know I could continue to eat and help Ruth. She was now in the Lutheran sanitarium in Denver. She would miss me, but she was well adjusted. It was a fine establishment that had been in business for some time and I did come out of the hills a few times a year.

I look at the pictures now and think, "My goodness, what an experience that was." The children seemed to be born on skis. I loved skiing and one of the big events, of course, was to go up to Steamboat Springs—I think in February—when they had the big-hill skiing event. People came there from all countries. I had never seen anything like it. The children did a beautiful job. There were street events in the morning and the youngsters were on their skis going through barrels that had the ends knocked out, and participating in potato races where they skied to the potatoes, speared the potato, and raced back to the starting point. The adults also had special races. One of them required the skier to ride behind a pony, hanging onto a rope—about forty feet of rope, I think, and while the pony galloped the skier had to take up the rope so that when he got to the end of the run he was supposed to be even with the pony and cross the line beside him. That took a little doing.

Ski Carnival at Steamboat Springs, Colorado, February 1939, through the barrel with skis on, according to the notation

Potato race

Cartoon characters on skis

For some reason or other, I guess I talked too much again and got myself in trouble. I was from Wisconsin, and I had done a little skiing, and I thought I knew a lot more than I did. The next thing I knew, about the second or third race, I pooh-poohed the stunt saying there was nothing to it. Then somebody tapped me on the shoulder and said, "Come on, you're the next rider behind the pony." I never saw the man before, but I'm sure a lot of my friends who were there with me knew who he was, and were probably tired of me talking so big. The man said, "I just talked to the guy that keeps coming in second and talked him into letting you ride instead of the rider he had already assigned." Well, this was a different story, but there was no backing down.

The next thing I knew I was at the end to that rope. He helped me buckle my skis onto my boots and gave me the rope. Somebody blew a whistle and away we went. I was really not prepared, not at all! We went sailing across the snow. The little pony was throwing snowballs off its little hooves going full gallop. Snow was filling my parka. My eyes were full of water. I was sweating, well, practically, blood. All of a sudden I realized I had to start taking up the rope so I could cross at the same time the horse did. I didn't know what to do with the rope when I took it up. I was afraid to drop it for fear I'd get it tangled in my skis. About the time I got in front of the people who had set me up for this, one ski hit a chunk and went up in the air and I was riding along full speed on one ski. I finally got it down on the snow again. We made it! We made it in the same record time as the skier I had replaced. We—the pony and I—got second place! Of course, it was announced over the radio. My sister who was down in Denver heard the announcement that Florence Taubman—my name wasn't King then—won second prize in the pony race. For my prize I was given a zipper purse. It was a boxy thing with two handles and two zippers. I should have kept it and mounted it or something because it was probably the only time I would ever win anything.

I still seem to have the talking problem, but I suppose that's going with me to the grave. I don't know. I hope it's useful at that time. That would be nice, wouldn't it? (The pony stunt is now called "Skijoring." They do many stunts and ride between flags, etc. It is a big sport and is trying for the Olympics, I read.)

EPILOGUE
The Golden Years

On one of the trips to Wisconsin I became engaged to a Wisconsin man, but returned to Colorado to do another year of teaching. Anyway, the tuberculosis thing interfered with that intent of marriage. His family couldn't tolerate the idea that I was responsible for the care of my ill sister and that there was too much TB in the family. One really couldn't blame them.

I went back to teaching in Wisconsin and eventually married Mr. King. I kept teaching after marriage. We adopted two children and had a good life. So all is well that ends well.

I was converted by the Dominicans and taught school for Notre Dame and had a personal friend in the Carmelites. And now I'm all eager about the Franciscans and their work.

I appreciate all the efforts that the nuns have put into my life. I also want to say that I don't believe I've emphasized enough that what I did for my sister reverts back to the Woodmen. My being in Colorado made it possible to, eventually, send for her. She lived with me in Kiowa and later went into the Lutheran Home in Denver. She had been in and out of institutions for years. She'd get run down and feel as if she was in trouble and would again enter a sanitarium for a few months to recuperate. Eventually the two of us were well enough to go back to Wisconsin where she married an older man and had a good life. She had a job in a small-town bakery, decorating cakes and mingling with people . She had her own income, which was a new experience for her. She lived well into her early seventies, which was really an achievement in those days.

*   *   *   *

As I think back now in my spare time, it's amazing to me to realize how important Woodmen had been, not only in my own life but in the life of my whole family, really, my parents and surely in the life of my sister who was tubercular. I can't get over how it took me so long to appreciate and recognize the significance of what took place in the thirties. When everything was going wrong, I had one thing going right for me, that's for sure. The Franciscans took over and are keeping the place beautiful and useful. It is a pleasure to me since I have now become familiar with Mother Angelica's program on TV and listen to their mass service every morning at 7:00 here. I feel as if I almost know them. I have been to their convent in LaCrosse also. I have a niece who teaches there. It is a beautiful campus. I think it would be most enjoyable if they would start taking in old women like me. It's a lucrative business, you know. I've found that out by being on the paying end of this Lutheran Institution here.

April 2000

Today was census day, and I really blew it. Went out when I should have stayed in. Ran smack into the big chief holding three long-form government papers, and she said, "Will you please do a long form? I've got three left to get rid of." I guess our group required seven long forms. What could I say?

As I returned to my apartment to start work on it, I remembered I hadn't filed income tax forms in at least ten years. You say I'm not in the computer, to which my reaction was, "Hooray!" So, from now on I am alive and an Iowa Citizen—car and driver license all on record. And my only hope is to die before the revenuers find me. The government employed assistant assured me it was an honor to be asked to do the long form! More government propaganda, but flattery will get you… (old ego at work).

November 2001

My son Dick is picking me up the 16th or 17th and returning me the 27th or 28th. Jere is putting a plate on their table for me—he's a doubting Thomas.

We had our annual Christmas party this P.M. at the Gernand Center in Strawberry Point, Iowa. We welcome all residents who have joined us since December 31, 2000. I'm on for welcoming all guests because I have a name for being the biggest idiot resident, and I pretty well live up to my reputation. We meet the honored guests, welcome them, put their name tags on and seat them in a row of uncomfortable chairs against the wall. There should have been eight, but one husband and wife were fortunate enough to have doctor's appointments out of town and another one was smart enough (after sitting there a half hour) to "feel ill" and go home. All "old" residents and employees, etc. were guided to the honored guests and then got their cake and coffee—silver urns, no less—and formed groups at various tables. Well, honored guests sat and watched. I advised them to change the system next year.

So much for the Christmas party. I entertained the best I could! I offered to sing but they thought better of it. We sing carols Monday from 11:00 to 11:30 A.M. They've heard me. I throw everyone off pitch, but I like to sing.

CHRISTMAS 2004

Why I Love Iowa
When it's Christmastime in Iowa
And the gentle breezes blow
About seventy miles an hour and it's fifty-two below,
You can tell you're in Iowa
Cause the snow's up to your butt
And you take a breath of Christmas air
And your nose holes both freeze shut.
The weather here is wonderful,
So I guess I'll hang around.
I could never, ever leave Iowa,
My feet are frozen to the ground.
(Florence King)

So anyway, I wish you all well and God bless. Bye-bye.

Florence relaxing at Beverly and Jere's, 2006

Ninety-fifth birthday, 2006

Florence with Jan Roys on the island of Taiwan, December 1996

Florence at Verneta's ninetieth birthday, May 1995

Florence, Mildred, and Verneta, May 1990

Verneta and Florence, 1979

Florence, Ruth, and Verneta at Shell Lake, 1978

Florence, Hedwig, Ruth, and Verneta, 1964

Ruth, Lawrence, Hedwig, Verneta, and Florence, 1963